APPLYING
THE BIBLE
TO LIFE

A 4-week course to help junior highers plug into the power of God's Word

by Paul Woods

Group

Loveland, Colorado

Group®

Applying the Bible to Life

Copyright © 1991 by Group Publishing, Inc.

Scripture quotations are from the Holy Bible, New International Version. Copyright © 1973, 1978, 1984 International Bible Society. Used by permission of Zondervan Bible Publishers.

Credits
Edited by Michael D. Warden
Cover designed by Jill Christopher and DeWain Stoll
Interior designed by Judy Atwood Bienick and Jan Aufdemberge
Illustrations by Raymond Medici

ISBN 1-55945-116-5

15 14 13 12 11 10   04 03 02 01 00 99 98
Printed in the United States of America.

CONTENTS

INTRODUCTION 4
Applying the Bible to Life

COURSE OBJECTIVES.....................5

HOW TO USE THIS COURSE............6

THIS COURSE AT A GLANCE............8

PUBLICITY PAGE 9

LESSON 1 11
A Word for Today
Help junior highers see how God guided the formation of the scriptures to deliver his message to us.

LESSON 2.............................20
A Handbook for Life
Help junior highers understand that the Bible is a handbook for life.

LESSON 3.............................28
But How Do I Find It?
Help junior highers learn to use Bible-study tools to understand the Bible better.

LESSON 4.............................36
Personal Bible Study
Help junior highers see the importance of personal Bible study and give them methods to use in doing it.

BONUS IDEAS 45

96923

INTRODUCTION

APPLYING THE BIBLE TO LIFE

The Bible is a big mystery to most junior highers and middle schoolers. And not a mystery they're too interested in investigating. It's just too "tough to read," "boring" or "hard to connect to the 'real' world."

But is it really? Absolutely not.

Part of the problem is perception. As advertising people tell us, "perception is reality" to most people. And since most junior highers perceive the Bible to be too tough, boring or irrelevant, they don't read it much.

Another part of the problem is adult Christians. The statistics on adults reading the Bible aren't much better than the statistics on teenagers reading the Bible. If kids don't see us adults studying the Bible and applying it to our lives, how can we expect them to do it?

So what do we do?

We start by giving kids a good example. We study God's Word regularly, and report to kids how God is working in our lives through his Word. We model what we want kids to do.

Then we start working on perception. We show kids how this book called the Bible came about. We point out to them the incredible fact that the creator of the universe cares to communicate with them. We help kids discover scripture pas-

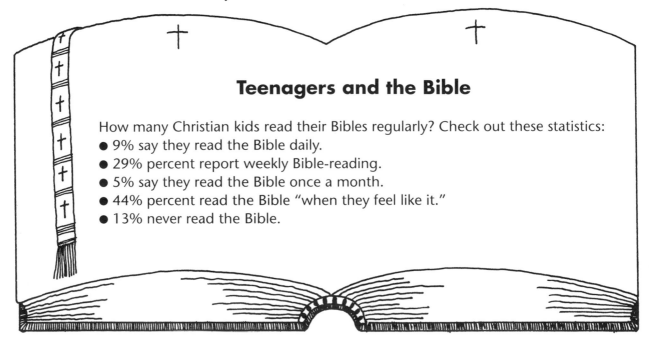

Teenagers and the Bible

How many Christian kids read their Bibles regularly? Check out these statistics:
- 9% say they read the Bible daily.
- 29% percent report weekly Bible-reading.
- 5% say they read the Bible once a month.
- 44% percent read the Bible "when they feel like it."
- 13% never read the Bible.

sages that relate to struggles they face. And we show kids how the Bible can make a difference in their lives.

The Bible is our guide. It helps us get to know God and build a relationship with him. And it helps us understand how we can please God. As kids begin to study and understand the Bible, they'll grow in their relationship with God and in their maturity as Christians.

This four-week course will help your junior highers and middle schoolers understand what the Bible is and what it can do for them. It'll challenge them to study the Bible more, and give them tools and methods they can use to study the Bible on their own. It'll encourage them to get to know God better through his revelation to people—the Bible.

And when kids make getting to know God a priority, the other parts of their lives will make more sense!

During this course your students will:
● see how God guided the formation of the scriptures to deliver his message to people;
● begin to see the Bible as a handbook for life;
● learn to use Bible-study tools to understand the Bible better;
● see the importance of personal Bible study; and
● learn a method for personal Bible study.

COURSE OBJECTIVES

HOW TO USE THIS COURSE

ACTIVE LEARNING

Think back on an important lesson you've learned in life. Did you learn it from reading about it? from hearing about it? from something you experienced? Chances are, the most important lessons you've learned came from something you experienced. That's what active learning is—learning by doing. And active learning is a key element in Group's Active Bible Curriculum.

Active learning leads students in doing things that help them understand important principles, messages and ideas. It's a discovery process that helps kids internalize what they learn.

Each lesson section in Group's Active Bible Curriculum plays an important part in active learning:

The **Opener** involves kids in the topic in fun and unusual ways.

The **Action and Reflection** includes an experience designed to evoke specific feelings in the students. This section also processes those feelings through "How did you feel?" questions and applies the message to situations kids face.

The **Bible Application** actively connects the topic with the Bible. It helps kids see how the Bible's message is relevant to the situations they face.

The **Commitment** helps students internalize the Bible's message and commit to make changes in their lives.

The **Closing** funnels the lesson's message into a time of creative reflection and prayer.

When you put all the sections together, you get a lesson that's fun to teach—and kids get messages they'll remember.

BEFORE THE 4-WEEK SESSION

● Read the Introduction, the Course Objectives and This Course at a Glance.

● Decide how you'll publicize the course using the clip art on the Publicity Page (p. 9). Prepare fliers, newsletter articles and posters as needed.

● Look at the Bonus Ideas (p. 45) and decide which ones you'll use.

● Read the opening statements, Objectives and Bible Basis for the lesson. The Bible Basis shows how specific passages relate to junior highers today.

● Choose which Opener and Closing options to use. Each is appropriate for a different kind of group. The first option is often more active.

● Gather necessary supplies listed in This Lesson at a Glance.

● Read each section of the lesson. Adjust where necessary for your class size and meeting room.

● The approximate minutes listed give you an idea of how long each activity will take. Each lesson is designed to take 35 to 60 minutes. Shorten or lengthen activities as needed to fit your group.

● If you see you're going to have extra time, do an activity or two from the "If You Still Have Time . . ." box or from the Bonus Ideas (p. 45).

● Dive into the activities with the kids. Don't be a spectator. The lesson will be more success-ful and rewarding to you and your students.

● The answers given after discussion ques-tions are responses your students *might* give. They aren't the only answers or the "right" answers. If needed, use them to spark dis-cussion. Kids won't always say what you wish they'd say. That's why some of the responses given are negative or controversial. If some-one responds negatively, don't be shocked. Accept the person, and use the opportunity to explore other angles of the issue.

THIS COURSE AT A GLANCE

Before you dive into the lessons, familiarize yourself with each lesson aim. Then read the scripture passages.
- Study them as a background to the lessons.
- Use them as a basis for your personal devotions.
- Think about how they relate to kids' circumstances today.

LESSON 1: A WORD FOR TODAY

Lesson Aim: To help junior highers see how God guided the formation of the scriptures to deliver his message to us.

Bible Basis: Deuteronomy 31:9-13 and John 20:30-31.

LESSON 2: A HANDBOOK FOR LIFE

Lesson Aim: To help junior highers understand that the Bible is a handbook for life.

Bible Basis: Psalm 119:105-106 and 2 Timothy 3:16-17.

LESSON 3: BUT HOW DO I FIND IT?

Lesson Aim: To help junior highers learn to use Bible-study tools to understand the Bible better.

Bible Basis: 2 Timothy 2:15 and 2 Peter 3:15-18.

LESSON 4: PERSONAL BIBLE STUDY

Lesson Aim: To help junior highers see the importance of personal Bible study and give them methods to use in doing it.

Bible Basis: Genesis 12:1-4; Daniel 6:10-11; and Matthew 14:13-14, 23.

PUBLICITY PAGE

G rab your junior highers' attention! Photocopy this page, then cut and paste the art of your choice in your church bulletin or newsletter to advertise this course on applying the Bible to life. Or photocopy and use the ready-made flier as a bulletin insert. Permission to photocopy this clip art is granted for local church use.

Splash this art on posters, fliers or even postcards! Just add the vital details: the date and time the course begins and where you'll meet.

It's that simple.

Applying the Bible to Life

A 4-week junior high course on understanding and using the Bible

Come to _____

On _____

At _____

Come learn where the Bible came from, and how it can help you get where you want to go!

A WORD FOR TODAY

Junior highers and middle schoolers often see the Bible as an old book that has little relevance to their lives. But though the Bible is old, it reveals God's message to us. And that message is timeless!

To help junior highers see how God guided the formation of the scriptures to deliver his message to us.

Students will:
- **explore why God gave us his message in writing;**
- **discover how much people needed God's guidance in determining what to include in the Bible;**
- **examine God's purpose in giving us the Bible; and**
- **commit to leaning on God's Word for help.**

LESSON AIM

OBJECTIVES

BIBLE BASIS
DEUTERONOMY 31:9-13
JOHN 20:30-31

Look up the following scriptures. Then read the background paragraphs to see how the passages relate to your junior highers or middle schoolers.

In **Deuteronomy 31:9-13**, Moses gave instructions about how God's Word was to be used.

Moses knew he'd die soon, so he wrote the things God had said to him, and told the people to have God's Word read to them regularly. In this way, future generations would learn about God and learn to obey his Word.

Kids today have God's Word readily available to them in written form, so they can read it whenever they want. But it seems they don't often want to. Through this passage, kids can see that the Bible isn't just a bunch of stories. It's God revealing himself to us.

In **John 20:30-31**, John tells us why he wrote about Jesus' life.

This passage implies why God revealed his Word through

John and the other Bible writers. God gave his Word so we would believe in Jesus.

The Bible was written for everyone. Sometimes young teenagers seem to think it's just for little kids and adults. But through the Bible, God reveals his message of eternal life in Christ, and that's something kids need to know about too.

THIS LESSON AT A GLANCE

Section	Minutes	What Students Will Do	Supplies
Opener (Option 1)	5 to 10	**Silent Message**—Convey a message to a partner without talking.	Pencils, paper, "Message Instructions" boxes (p. 13)
(Option 2)		**Making Sure**—Recite the definition of the word "sure" from memory.	Dictionary, newsprint, marker
Action and Reflection	15 to 20	**Who Says?**—Choose which statements from a list are found in the Bible.	Pencils, "And God Said . . ." handouts (p. 17)
Bible Application	10 to 15	**On Purpose**—Create presentations that show why God gave us the Bible.	Bibles, newsprint, markers, treats
Commitment	5 to 10	**Help Along the Way**—Find ways to use the Bible in everyday life.	Newsprint, marker
Closing (Option 1)	up to 5	**Celebrate the Scriptures**—Participate in a group cheer for God.	"Three Cheers for God" handouts (p. 18)
(Option 2)		**The Bible for This Week**—Receive a Bible-reading plan for the week.	"Scripture Readings" bookmarks (p. 16)

The Lesson

OPENER
(5 to 10 minutes)

☐ OPTION 1: SILENT MESSAGE

Before class, place pencils and sheets of paper around the room. When kids arrive, form pairs. Give one partner in each pair a photocopy of the "Message Instructions" from the box on page 13. Have that partner follow the instructions to get the message to the other partner.

Give kids a few minutes to communicate the message. Then ask:

● **How did you communicate your message without speaking?** (Wrote it; used gestures.)

● **Which method of communication was most accurate?** (Writing it.)

Say: **Today we're going to study an important message that's also been communicated to us in writing. The message comes from God working through human writers. The message tells us God's plan for making our lives the best they can be.**

☐ **OPTION 2: MAKING SURE**

Bring a full-size dictionary to class. Write the word "sure" on a sheet of newsprint. As kids enter, have them take turns looking up the definition of "sure" in the dictionary. Warn kids not to tell each other what they found.

After at least five kids—or all kids if you have fewer than eight—have looked up the word, get the dictionary and ask:

● **What's the definition of "sure"? Try to give it to me word for word.**

After several volunteers attempt to give you the definition, ask:

● **Why do we have so many variations of the definition?** (We all remember different things; there's too much to remember.)

● **What would happen to our language if there were no dictionaries?** (Words might mean different things to different people; we'd never remember everything.)

● **Why do you think God had people write his message to us in the Bible?** (So we wouldn't get confused; to keep it from getting changed.)

Say: **Writing something is the *sure* way to pass a message along to several people. If it's written, a message doesn't get changed when people forget parts of it. And that's probably why God chose to have his message to us written by people who loved him.**

In the next four weeks we're going to examine God's message for us—the Bible—and learn how it can guide us through life.

WHO SAYS?

Form groups of about three, and give kids each a "And God Said . . ." handout (p. 17). Have groups each discuss the statements on the handout and decide which ones are from the Bible.

As kids discuss the statements, go around from group to group and give them hints to help them decide which statements are really from the Bible. The correct answers are in the "Biblical-Statement Answers" box on page 14.

After groups finish their handouts, discuss which statements really are from the Bible.

Message Instructions

Communicate the message below to your partner. But there's one catch: You may not speak!

God loves you and has big plans for your life.

ACTION AND REFLECTION
(15 to 20 minutes)

Biblical-Statement Answers

1. Herman Melville
2. Rousseau
3. Ecclesiastes 7:8a
4. Hugh Black
5. Thomas Carlyle
6. Psalm 68:2a
7. Proverbs 9:17
8. Pascal
9. Matthew 10:24
10. Paul Scherer
11. Song of Songs 8:7a

Then ask:

● **Why was it so hard to decide which statements are from the Bible?** (They all sounded alike; I didn't know some of that stuff was in the Bible.)

● **How did it feel not knowing which ones to choose?** (Frustrating; not too bad.)

● **How is that like the way the early Christians might've felt as they tried to decide what to include in the New Testament?** (They must've felt even more overwhelmed; they were probably frustrated too.)

● **How did you feel when I came around and helped you?** (Relieved; more confident of our answers.)

● **How was that like how the early Christians might've felt, knowing the Holy Spirit was guiding them to form the Bible?** (Good; confident; like it wasn't all on their shoulders.)

Have kids sit in chairs in a circle. Say: **I'm going to read some information about the Bible. Listen as I read, and every time I say something you don't already know, move one space to the right.**

Read this aloud: **It probably wasn't easy for the early Christians to decide which books God wanted in the New Testament. By that time, the Old Testament—the part of the Bible written before Jesus came—was already written and accepted by God's people.**

But deciding what should be included in the New Testament was hard. Lots of books and letters had been written by Christians in the first 100 years after Christ. And not all of them belonged in the Bible. So in the second century after Christ, the Christians came up with four basic questions to guide them in selecting which books and letters should be included in the Bible:

1. Was the book or letter written or approved by an apostle?

2. Were its contents essentially spiritual?

3. Did the book or letter show evidence of being inspired by God?

4. Had most churches accepted it?

These questions made deciding easier. But even with God's guidance, it still took around 200 more years to settle the issue. The Bible was finally certified as complete by a council of church leaders in A.D. 397. And it's still the same today!

After the reading, have kids return to their original chairs. Say: **As we can see, there's a lot we don't know about how the Bible was formed. But God made sure the Bible came to us as he wanted it to, because he has a special purpose for it. Let's look at what that purpose is.**

ON PURPOSE

Form three groups. A group can be one person. Assign one of these passages to each group: Deuteronomy 31:9-13; John 20:30-31; and 2 Timothy 3:15-16.

Say: **We're going to have a contest. The winner will be the group that can tell most accurately what the purpose of the Bible is. You have five minutes to prepare your presentations.**

Let groups each choose how to make their presentation. Suggest options such as a news report, a scientific announcement, a visual presentation using newsprint and markers, or a skit. After five minutes, have groups give their presentations.

Then ask:

● **Which of these Bible purposes is correct?**

Write kids' responses on newsprint. All purposes the kids present will likely be correct. If so, congratulate them all, and award each student a treat you know kids like, such as a doughnut or candy bar. But tell kids they can't eat their treats for a few minutes. Read aloud the groups' answers again, and ask:

● **So why did God give us the Bible?** (To help us learn about him; to help us believe in Jesus; to help us find eternal life.)

● **I gave you treats, but you haven't eaten them yet. How do you know they'll be good?** (Because I trust you; because of the name on the wrapper.)

● **How is believing your treat is good like believing the Bible is good?** (God gave us the Bible, and we can trust him; if it's God's Word, it must be good.)

Let kids eat their treats as you begin the next activity.

HELP ALONG THE WAY

Say: **Knowing we can trust the Bible as God's message for us makes the Bible extremely important to us. Let's list some ways God might want us to use the Bible to help us.**

Have kids brainstorm ways to use the Bible as you write their ideas on newsprint. If they have trouble getting started, give them a few suggestions; for example, "to find answers to our problems," "to let God teach us through it" or "to guide us in making decisions about relationships."

When you've listed five or six things, form pairs. Say: **Discuss with your partner ways each of you can gain more help from the Bible. Then choose one particular way to use the Bible this week.**

After a few minutes, say: **After you've each determined how you'll apply the Bible's message to your life this week, shake hands and tell each other something you admire about the other person's plans for using the Bible. For example, you might say, "I think it's neat that you're going to look in the Bible for guidance about school."**

COMMITMENT
(5 to 10 minutes)

Table Talk

The Table Talk activity in this course helps junior highers and middle schoolers discuss with their parents how to apply the Bible to their lives.

If you choose to use the Table Talk activity, this is a good time to show students the "Table Talk" handout (p. 19). Ask them to spend time with their parents completing it.

Before kids leave, give them each the "Table Talk" handout to take home, or tell them you'll send it to their parents.

Or use the Table Talk idea found in the Bonus Ideas (p. 45) for a meeting based on the handout.

CLOSING
(up to 5 minutes)

Scripture Readings

Monday:
Luke 15:1-10

Tuesday:
Acts 2:14-39

Wednesday:
Proverbs 4

Thursday:
Matthew 7:24-27

Friday:
Psalm 121

Saturday:
Romans 12

☐ OPTION 1: CELEBRATE THE SCRIPTURES

To wrap up your lesson, give kids each a "Three Cheers for God" handout (p. 18) and assign parts to them. It's okay if more than one person has the same part; just have them read in unison. Have kids read aloud through the handout to celebrate what God has given us in his Word.

☐ OPTION 2: THE BIBLE FOR THIS WEEK

Give kids photocopies of the "Scripture Readings" bookmark in the margin. Say: **If we want help from the Bible, we have to read it. If you aren't already reading the Bible regularly, get started on these passages this week.**

Close the lesson with prayer, asking God to help your kids use the Bible to help them this week.

If You Still Have Time . . .

In God We Trust—Form groups of about three. Have groups each come up with a slogan that tells why we should believe God's Word. Then have groups each use posterboard and markers to create a poster presenting their slogan. When kids are finished, have groups each present their poster, and tape it to the wall. Leave the posters up throughout this course on the Bible. Then display them for the rest of the congregation to see.

Bible Quiz—Form two groups. Have each group come up with three questions about the Bible based on today's lesson. Then have groups take turns asking each other their questions. Judge the correctness of the answers, and congratulate the team that gives the most correct answers. For extra fun, do the quiz *Jeopardy* style, having groups each come up with answers the other group must discover questions for.

AND GOD SAID...

Some of the statements below are from the Bible. Others are from people throughout history. Checkmark all those you think are from the Bible.

1. He offered a prayer so deeply devout that he seemed kneeling and praying at the bottom of the sea. ☐

2. Do not judge, and you will never be mistaken. ☐

3. The end of a matter is better than its beginning, and patience is better than pride. ☐

4. The fear of God kills all other fears. ☐

5. Blessed are the valiant that have lived in the Lord. ☐

6. As smoke is blown away by the wind, may you blow them away. ☐

7. Stolen water is sweet; food eaten in secret is delicious! ☐

8. It is the heart which experiences God, and not the reason. ☐

9. A student is not above his teacher, nor a servant above his master. ☐

10. We find freedom when we find God; we lose it when we lose him. ☐

11. Many waters cannot quench love; rivers cannot wash it away. ☐

THREE CHEERS FOR GOD

Read aloud the following prayer to celebrate all God has given us through his Word.

Reader 1: Lord, your Word is everlasting.

Reader 2: It continues forever in heaven.

All: Thanks, God, for giving us the Bible.

Reader 3: Your loyalty will continue from now on.

Reader 4: You made the Earth and it still stands.

All: Thanks, God, that we can trust in your Word.

Reader 1: All things continue to this day because of your laws.

Reader 2: All things serve you.

All: Thanks, God, for caring about us.

Reader 3: We will never forget your orders,

Reader 4: Because they fill us with life.

Readers 1 and 4: Thanks, God for telling us who you are.

All: Three cheers for God!

This reading is a paraphrase of Psalm 119:89-91, 93.

Table Talk

To the Parent: This month we're studying the Bible and what it means to us. Please take time to sit down with your junior higher or middle schooler to talk about the Bible. Use this sheet to guide your discussion.

Junior higher

Tell your parent what you've discovered so far in the course on the Bible.

Parent

Tell your junior higher what you've learned about the Bible throughout your life. Tell about specific times it's been particularly helpful to you.

Parent and junior higher

● Tell what the Bible means to you.

● Read 2 Timothy 3:14-17 together and discuss what it means.

● Discuss what your pattern of personal Bible study is and what you'd like it to be.

● Work out a plan to support and encourage each other in personal Bible study. Be sure to include times of telling each other what you've gained from your study.

● If you don't already have family devotions, talk together about how you might start them. And set a day for the first one. To help you get started, get a copy of *Fun Devotions for Parents and Teenagers* (Family Tree). It's got 52 lively devotions that focus on applying the Bible to life.

APPLYING
THE BIBLE
TO LIFE

LESSON 2

A HANDBOOK FOR LIFE

Most junior highers and middle schoolers probably see the Bible as a religious object to be respected and treated with great care. But God wants the Bible to be a guide or handbook for life. God's Word is designed to be applied to everyday circumstances. Not until kids dig into the pages of the Bible will they discover the truths that can lead them to abundant life.

LESSON AIM

To help junior highers understand that the Bible is a handbook for life.

OBJECTIVES

Students will:
● examine what handbooks do for us;
● experience the advantages of having something to guide us;
● discover how the Bible can guide us in our lives;
● seek God's help in finding guidance from the Bible; and
● thank God for guiding us through his Word.

BIBLE BASIS
PSALM 119:105-106
2 TIMOTHY 3:16-17

Look up the following scriptures. Then read the background paragraphs to see how the passages relate to your junior highers or middle schoolers.

In **Psalm 119:105-106**, the psalmist uses an analogy of a lamp to describe God's Word.

This passage shows how the Bible can give light to our lives the way a floodlight lights the way on a path. Sometimes it's hard to know what we should do; we have to function "in the dark." But God's Word can help us see what's best for us.

Young teenagers today face a lot of unknowns—places where they're "in the dark." The Bible can give them guidance to help them along the path of adolescence.

In **2 Timothy 3:16-17**, Paul explains the value of the scriptures.

Paul points out that the Bible isn't just another book, but is given by the breath of God. It's not just a book to read and think about but to help us live lives pleasing to God.

Junior highers may think the Bible is an old book of rules. But it's a book God gave us to help us live for him. By helping kids study and apply God's Word to their lives, we'll help kids prepare to serve God the best way they can.

THIS LESSON AT A GLANCE

Section	Minutes	What Students Will Do	Supplies
Opener (Option 1)	5 to 10	**Class Acts**—Create a handbook for new class members.	Paper, stapler, markers
(Option 2)		**By the Book**—Describe the purposes of different types of handbooks.	Handbooks, markers, background music, stereo
Action and Reflection	10 to 15	**The Hunt**—Compete in a search for hidden treasure.	Gold-coin candy or something similar, "Treasure Map" handout (p. 26), "Treasure Instructions" handout (p. 27), pencil
Bible Application	10 to 15	**Light in the Darkness**—Write a prescription for sending God's light into a dark spot in someone's life.	Desk lamp, Bibles, paper, pencils
Commitment	10 to 15	**Shine on Me**—Write areas in their lives that need God's light.	Paper, pencils, Bibles, desk lamp
Closing (Option 1)	up to 5	**Stating the Case**—Create slogans about how the Bible can help people.	Paper, markers, tape
(Option 2)		**The Word From the Word**—Report on private Bible-reading from the previous week.	"Scripture Readings 2" bookmarks (p. 25)

The Lesson

☐ OPTION 1: CLASS ACTS

Form groups of three or four. Give groups each a sheet of paper and some markers. Have them fold their paper twice, once each way. Then staple along the crease of the last fold and cut off the other fold, creating an eight-page booklet (see example on page 22). Have groups each quickly create a New-Member Handbook for your class. Tell them to put in it every-

OPENER
(5 to 10 minutes)

thing they can think of that someone new coming in should know about the class. If groups write one item on each page after the title page, they'll have room for six or seven items.

When groups have finished, have them each report what they put in their handbook.

Then ask:

● **What good is a handbook?** (It gives us guidelines; it helps us know how to act.)

Say: **Today we're going to look at the Bible as a kind of handbook—a handbook for living lives that please God.**

☐ OPTION 2: BY THE BOOK

Before the lesson, collect handbooks from cars, appliances, video equipment or other items you have around the house. Number each handbook. When kids arrive, have them pass the books around to look at.

After about a minute, start playing music. Then stop the music, and have the person holding handbook 1 briefly explain what that handbook does. Then start the music again and have kids pass around the handbooks. Stop the music again and have the person holding handbook 2 describe it. Do the same until you've covered all the handbooks.

Then ask:

● **What good are handbooks?** (They give you instructions; they help you know what to do and what not to do.)

Say: **We've looked at several different kinds of handbooks already, but today we're going to look at a different kind of handbook—the Bible. It's our handbook for learning to live lives pleasing to God.**

Table Talk Follow-Up

If you sent the "Table Talk" handout (p. 19) to parents last week, discuss students' reactions to the activity. Ask volunteers to tell what they learned from the discussions with their parents.

THE HUNT

Before class, carefully hide a treasure, such as a bag of gold-coin candy or something else kids could share, somewhere in or near your meeting room. Be sure it's not too easy to find.

Photocopy the "Treasure Map" handout (p. 26) and "Treasure Instructions" handout (p. 27). On the "Treasure Map" handout, draw a simple map showing precisely where the treasure is, and describe it. Don't write or draw anything on the "Treasure Instructions" handout. Fold both handouts in half.

Form two teams. Tell kids they're going on a treasure hunt. Say: **The team that finds the treasure first gets to keep it. Your instructions are secret. Don't let the other team see your instructions.**

Give one team the "Treasure Map" handout and the other team the "Treasure Instructions" handout. Have teams each look for the treasure.

The team with the map should find the treasure quickly. The other team may quickly complain about the unfairness of the hunt. Let the complaining go on for a bit, then bring the group together for discussion.

Ask:

● **Why was it so easy for one group to find the treasure?** (They had a map; they knew what the treasure was.)

● **Why was it harder for the other group?** (We didn't have any instructions; we had no idea where to look.)

● **What did the map and the description do for the winning group?** (It helped them know what they were looking for; they knew exactly where to look.)

● **How is the treasure map in this activity like the Bible in our lives?** (They both help us find our way; they both help us know what to look for.)

Say: **The Bible was written to be kind of like a treasure map—a handbook to help us find and build a relationship with God. Now let's look at what God says about how we're to use the Bible.**

Give the losing team a "good sport" treasure—one just like the winning team's treasure.

LIGHT IN THE DARKNESS

Plug in and turn on the desk lamp you brought to class. Then ask one of your students to sit by the desk lamp and read aloud Psalm 119: 102-108. As the person begins reading, turn off the other lights in the room and darken it as much as possible. As soon as the student completes verse 105, turn off the lamp. The student may be able to finish reading, depending on how dark the room is.

When the student is finished or stops, ask:

● **What did the lamp do for the person reading?** (It gave him light; it helped her see the words.)

● **What happened when I turned off the lamp?** (It got dark; it made it hard to read.)

● **In this passage, the psalmist is comparing God's Word to a lamp. How is the Bible like a lamp for us?** (It helps us see where we're going; it helps us see where we are.)

Say: **God has given us the Bible to help us find our way—like a lamp in the darkness. Now let's see just how it does that.**

Form pairs, and give pairs each a sheet of paper, a pencil and a Bible. Say: **Each pair is a team of doctors. Your patient is the person described in 2 Timothy 3:17, but that patient isn't well—not able to do "every good work." Your job is to prescribe the medicine the patient needs to survive. You'll find that medicine in 2 Timothy 3:16.**

Have pairs each write their recommendations.

Ask:

● **What's your recommended prescription?** (Teaching; learning what's wrong; learning how to live right.)

● **How can these prescriptions help us?** (They help us see when we do wrong; they tell us what we need to know to do what's right.)

● **How would trying to live for God without the Bible be like walking down an unfamiliar path in the dark?** (Both would be very tough; I'd stumble a lot either way.)

Say: **God's Word lights our paths. It helps us find our way, but only if we let it.**

Have partners each congratulate each other on a good diagnosis and a healthy patient by gently patting each other on the back as they speak.

COMMITMENT
(10 to 15 minutes)

SHINE ON ME

Distribute paper, pencils and Bibles. Have kids re-read 2 Timothy 3:16-17.

Say: **We've seen several ways in this passage that God uses the Bible to help us. Take a hard look at these verses and pick out one area where you feel you need more of God's light. For example, you might need more of God's light in a relationship or in your decisions about the future. On your paper, write the area you choose.**

When kids finish writing, have them each fold their paper in half. Then turn on the lamp you used earlier and have kids each place their paper at the base of the lamp to symbolize receiving God's light in their lives. Encourage kids to pray silently as they bring their papers, asking God to help them find help in the Bible for their problem areas.

☐ OPTION 1: STATING THE CASE

Form groups of three or four. Tell groups they'll each write a slogan about how the Bible can help in their lives. Give kids paper and markers. Encourage them to come up with catchy phrases such as "Warm yourself in the sonlight of God's Word" or "The Bible: Read it, learn it, live it!"

When groups are ready, let them each present their slogan. Tape the slogans to your meeting-room walls, and leave them up for the remainder of the course.

End your lesson with prayer, letting volunteers thank God for his Word.

☐ OPTION 2: THE WORD FROM THE WORD

Let kids report what they learned from their Bible-reading this week. Be ready to report on your own reading too. Encourage kids who haven't tried Bible-reading to begin this week with the Bible passages in the "Scripture Readings 2" bookmark in the margin.

Wrap up your session with prayer. Pray that God's Word would be especially meaningful to your kids in the coming week.

CLOSING
(up to 5 minutes)

Scripture Readings 2

Monday:
Matthew 10:32-39

Tuesday:
John 6:35-51

Wednesday:
Psalm 119:9-16

Thursday:
Philippians 2:1-15

Friday:
Ecclesiastes 12:1-7

Saturday:
Matthew 25:31-46

Permission to photocopy this bookmark granted for local church use. Copyright © Group Publishing, Inc., Box 481, Loveland, CO 80539.

If You Still Have Time . . .

Living in the Light—Light a candle in a holder, and set it where all kids can see it. Turn off other room lights, and have kids look silently at the candle for one full minute. While they look, ask them to think about how Jesus gave light to the world, and how God's Word still gives "light" to our lives. Then have kids tell what they thought of.

Light of the World—Have kids each don a blindfold and perform several simple tasks, such as writing a note, pouring a glass of water, shaking hands with another person or arranging chairs in a circle. Then have kids each remove their blindfold and say how life would be different without light. Compare kids' answers to how their lives would be without the light of God's Word to guide them.

Treasure Map

Follow the map below to find the hidden treasure.

Treasure Instructions

Look around the area to find a treasure.

LESSON 3

BUT HOW DO I FIND IT?

Few junior highers and middle schoolers really dig into the Bible on a regular basis. One reason is that they have a hard time finding what they're looking for. Some simple Bible-study tools can help your kids find all the powerful messages God has for them in his Word.

LESSON AIM

To help junior highers learn to use Bible-study tools to understand the Bible better.

OBJECTIVES

Students will:
- examine how random searching through scriptures seldom meets their needs;
- experience how tough it can be to find answers to their questions;
- use Bible-study tools to help them understand scripture passages better; and
- discover biblical answers to their questions.

BIBLE BASIS
2 TIMOTHY 2:15
2 PETER 3:15-18

Look up the following scriptures. Then read the background paragraphs to see how the passages relate to your junior highers or middle schoolers.

In **2 Timothy 2:15**, Paul reminds Timothy of the importance of God's Word.

In this passage, Paul says that pleasing God involves correctly handling his Word. To do that, we need to study and understand it.

A big book like the Bible can bewilder junior highers. But they can learn to "correctly handle" it with a little help from you and from some simple Bible-study tools.

In **2 Peter 3:15-18**, Peter talks about the value of scripture in our lives.

The Bible came to us from God through his servants. Sometimes things in the Bible can be tough to understand, but they can help us keep on the right track. As we study the Bible and understand it better, we'll grow in our relationship with Christ.

Kids need a guide to keep them from error, just like the Christians of Peter's day did. As kids learn how they can understand the Bible better, they'll be better equipped to apply the Bible's truths to their lives, and grow in their relationship with Jesus.

THIS LESSON AT A GLANCE

Section	Minutes	What Students Will Do	Supplies
Opener (Option 1)	5 to 10	**Random Reading**—Randomly pick verses to answer specific questions.	Paper, pencils, Bibles
(Option 2)		**Bursting Balloons**—Burst balloons to discover the wrong way to find answers in the Bible.	"Scary Scriptures" box (p. 30), scissors, balloons
Action and Reflection	15 to 20	**Tough Questions**—Find answers to a quiz using various reference tools.	"Tough Trivia" handouts (p. 34), dictionary, newspaper, pencils
Bible Application	15 to 20	**Tools of the Trade**—Use Bible-study tools to find and examine specific Bible passages.	Biblical reference books, "What Do I Do With This?" handout (p. 35), Bibles, paper, pencils
Commitment	5 to 10	**Finding God's Answers**—Find biblical answers to specific questions.	Paper, pencils, Bibles, biblical reference books
Closing (Option 1)	up to 5	**Mystery Prayer**—Find and read the Lord's Prayer.	Bibles, biblical reference books
(Option 2)		**Tool Chart**—Create a chart outlining what to use specific Bible-study tools for.	3×5 cards, markers, "What Do I Do With This?" handout (p. 35)

The Lesson

☐ OPTION 1: RANDOM READING

As kids arrive, give them each a sheet of paper and a pencil. Have them each write a question they'd like the Bible to answer. Let kids know they'll be reading their questions to the class.

OPENER
(5 to 10 minutes)

When everyone is finished, hand out Bibles, and say: **Now let's find biblical answers to our questions. Close your eyes, open your Bible and point to a spot on the page you open to.**

Have kids each read their question and then read the verse they pointed to.

Ask:

● **How well did the verses answer the questions?** (Not at all; not too badly.)

● **Does this seem like a good way to find answers in the Bible? Explain.** (No, that's not how we should do it; no, it usually doesn't work this way.)

Say: **There are much better ways to find answers in the Bible. Today we'll look at tools that can help us find the answers we need.**

Collect the questions to use in the Finding God's Answers section.

☐ OPTION 2: BURSTING BALLOONS

Be sensitive to kids' feelings when deciding whether to do this activity. If there's recently been a suicide in your community, you may prefer to use Option 1.

Before class, photocopy and cut apart the "Scary Scriptures" from the box in the margin. Roll up the scriptures, and insert each one in a different-color balloon. Then blow up and tie the balloons.

To begin your class, distribute the balloons. Say: **Have you ever just opened your Bible and had it fall open to a scripture that really helped you? Sometimes that happens, but it's not always the best way to find answers. Suppose you are really depressed, and open your Bible for help. The first passage you find is Matthew 27:5.**

Have kids pop the balloons, and have the one with Matthew 27:5 read it aloud. Then say: **Now you flip a few more pages and your eyes fall on Luke 10:37b.**

Have the student with that slip read it aloud. When kids have stopped laughing, say: **That Bible-study approach didn't accomplish much, did it? Today we're going to discover better approaches to Bible study—ones that'll help us find what we need.**

Scary Scriptures

So Judas threw the money into the temple and left. Then he went away and hanged himself (Matthew 27:5).

Go and do likewise (Luke 10:37b).

TOUGH QUESTIONS

Form groups of three or four. Give each group a "Tough Trivia" handout (p. 34). Tell kids they have three minutes to find all the answers. Allow them to use a dictionary, yesterday's newspaper and any other reference tools you brought.

After three minutes, call time and give the answers from the "Answers to Tough Trivia" box in the margin. Have groups each report how many questions they answered correctly.

Then ask:

● **How tough was it to find the answers?** (Easy, we just didn't have time; hard, we didn't know where to look.)

● **What tools did you use to help you find the answers?** (The dictionary; the newspaper.)

● **How is finding those answers like finding answers in the Bible?** (Sometimes you just don't know where to look; it seems like answers you're looking for just aren't there.)

● **What tools might one use to help find answers in the Bible?** (A concordance; a Bible dictionary.)

If kids have trouble answering the last question, start holding up some of the Bible-study tools you brought to class.

Then say: **There are several tools that can help us find what we're looking for in the Bible. Let's look at a few of the most helpful ones.**

TOOLS OF THE TRADE

Pass around a Bible concordance (one found in the back of a Bible would work fine), a study Bible or a Bible commentary, and a Bible dictionary or encyclopedia. Check with your pastor to find these books. Or contact a local library to see if it has any available. If you have more than 10 kids, consider bringing more than one example of each.

Give kids Bibles and "What Do I Do With This?" handouts (p. 35) Briefly review the handout with your kids.

Say: **To get us started using these Bible-study tools, I'm going to let you find the passages we'll study today. I'll give you hints and let you use the tools we have here to find the scriptures.**

Give the following hints as needed until kids find the verses on their own. The hints are based on the New International Version of the Bible. If you use a different version, adjust your hints to fit your version. If kids have trouble deciding which tool to use, suggest they start with a concordance. But don't give them the references.

● **2 Timothy 2:15 hints:**
(a) contains the word "worker" or "workman"
(b) contains the word "true" or "truth"

Answers to Tough Trivia

1. (Check yesterday's newspaper.)
2. 1799
3. Walter Mondale
4. 5280
5. (Check local TV listings.)
6. a fictitious name
7. Asia
8. Tennessee Valley Authority
9. abacus
10. 1/12

BIBLE APPLICATION
(15 to 20 minutes)

(c) is in the New Testament

(d) is in one of the books Paul wrote

(e) is in 2 Timothy

(f) starts out "Do your best to present yourself to God as one approved . . ."

● **2 Peter 3:15-18 hints:**

(a) contains the word "scriptures"

(b) contains the word "Paul"

(c) is in the New Testament

(d) is in one of the books Peter wrote

(e) is in 2 Peter

(f) starts out "Bear in mind that our Lord's patience means salvation . . ."

When kids have tracked down the verses, form two groups. If you have more than 10 kids, form enough groups so you have no more than five kids in each group. Have each group study one of the two passages.

Say: **In your group, read your passage and discuss what it means. Then use the tools we have here to find out more about your passage. Record your findings on paper.**

Be sure each group has access to the Bible-study tools mentioned on the "What Do I Do With This?" handout. Give groups each paper and pencils. Then let them search for about 10 minutes. Circulate around the room, giving suggestions to groups having trouble.

After 10 minutes, have groups report what they found. Then ask:

● **What's the main message of 2 Timothy 2:15?** (It's important to understand what's in the Bible; God will be pleased if we study his Word well.)

● **What's the main message of 2 Peter 2:15-18?** (The words of scripture are from God; some things are hard to understand.)

● **How did the tools you used help you understand the scriptures better?** (They gave us new information; they helped us understand phrases that weren't clear to us.)

Say: **These tools can help us understand scripture. Now we're going to see if we can find answers to questions you have.**

COMMITMENT
(5 to 10 minutes)

FINDING GOD'S ANSWERS

If you used the Random Reading option for an opener, use the questions kids came up with then for this activity. If not, ask kids each to write on paper one question they'd like to find an answer for in the Bible. Then gather the questions.

Sort through the questions and choose some that kids are most likely to find answers to, using the tools you've provided. Choose one question for every four or five kids.

Form groups of four or five. Give each group one question to answer from the Bible. If kids have trouble finding answers, give suggestions. You may want to point out that some questions don't have easy answers—even when we have Bible-study tools to help us. Tell kids they may find principles to apply to specific situations instead of exact answers. Discuss briefly how the Bible's principles can apply to today's concerns.

Let groups work a few minutes, then have each group report.

After groups have reported, have kids in each group stand in a circle and put their arms around each other. Have kids each tell the person across from them one truth from the Bible that applies to him or her. For example, kids might say "God loves you" or "God has a plan for your life." Be sure each person is included.

☐ OPTION 1: MYSTERY PRAYER

Say: **To close our lesson, we're going to read a prayer together. But first you have to find that prayer. It's the prayer Jesus used in teaching his disciples how to pray. It's commonly known as the Lord's Prayer.**

Give kids Bibles and have the Bible-study materials available for them to use. Give hints as needed to help kids find the Lord's Prayer (Matthew 6:9-13 or Luke 11:2-4). When kids have found the prayer, read it together as your closing.

☐ OPTION 2: TOOL CHART

Form groups of two or three. Hand out 3×5 cards and markers. Have groups each use the information on the "What Do I Do With This?" handout to make a mini-chart to help them know which tools to use when they want to find something in the Bible. For example, kids can write where to look for a name, a particular word, a particular verse or a block of background information. Be sure each student makes a chart.

When kids are finished, have them each explain their chart. Then close with prayer.

CLOSING
(up to 5 minutes)

If You Still Have Time . . .

Library Tour—Go to a public library or your church library to look at tools kids can use in Bible study. Encourage kids to commit to use the tools when they want to find something. If possible, have the librarian tell about checkout procedures. Check some books out if kids want to.

Find-It-in-the-Bible Contest—Form two teams. Give a set of Bible tools to each team. Call out each subject below, but don't give the references. The first team to begin reading the correct passage from the Bible wins.

The subjects:
- Daniel in the lions' den (Daniel 6:16-24);
- David and Goliath (1 Samuel 17);
- The Sermon on the Mount (Matthew 5—7);
- Jesus' Resurrection (John 20:1-18);
- Noah and the flood (Genesis 6:9—9:19);
- The stoning of Stephen (Acts 7:54-60);
- Manna (Exodus 16); and
- Peter walking on water (Matthew 14:28-31).

TOUGH TRIVIA

1. What was the official high temperature the day before yesterday?

2. What year did George Washington die?

3. Who was vice president under Jimmy Carter?

4. How many feet are in a mile?

5. What TV show was on NBC at 9:00 last night?

6. What's a pseudonym?

7. Of the seven continents, which is largest in area?

8. What does TVA stand for?

9. What's a Chinese counting device made up of beads that slide on wires?

10. What proportion of a pound is a troy ounce?

WHAT DO I DO WITH THIS?

The following tools can help you study the Bible. Read through this sheet to see how each tool can help you, then keep this sheet handy at home for future reference.

Bible Concordance

What it does—A concordance lists words from the Bible in alphabetical order, then tells where those words appear in the Bible. Some big, full-book concordances contain every word in every verse of the Bible. Others, such as those in the back of many Bibles, contain only the most significant words in verses.

How you can use it—You can use a concordance for at least two purposes. One is to find places in the Bible where a particular word is used. For example, if you want to read verses that mention "sin," look up "sin" in your concordance, then look up the Bible references listed there.

Concordances can also help you find passages you "kind of" know but aren't sure where they are. For example, if you remember a verse that says something about God loving the world but don't know where to find it, you can look up "love" in your concordance. If you remember other words from the verse, you can look them up too. Before long you'll track down your verse: John 3:16.

Bible Dictionary or Encyclopedia

What it does—A Bible dictionary or encyclopedia lists biblical topics, people and places in alphabetical order. For each item listed, it gives historical information and explains the topics to help you understand the Bible better.

How you can use it—You can use a Bible dictionary to help you learn about people, places or things in the Bible. For example, suppose you want to find out who the Apostle Paul was. You can look up "Paul" in a Bible dictionary and it'll provide information about who Paul was and what he did.

A Study Bible or Bible Commentary

What it does—A study Bible or Bible commentary follows scripture and gives comments to help us understand passages and words in the Bible. A study Bible usually covers the whole Bible. A commentary may cover the whole Bible, only the Old or New Testament, or even just one Bible book.

How you can use it—You can use study Bibles or Bible commentaries to help you understand parts of scripture. For example, if you're not sure what Jesus means in John 4:10 when he talks about "living water," you could look up that verse in a study Bible or commentary to help you understand.

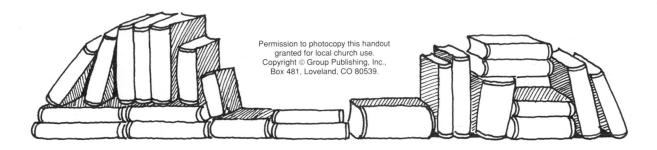

PERSONAL BIBLE STUDY

Some kids don't study the Bible on their own because they don't understand its importance. Others neglect Bible study because they don't know how to go about it. This session will help both of those kinds of kids see what's so great about the Bible and learn how to study it on their own.

LESSON AIM

To help junior highers see the importance of personal Bible study and give them methods to use in doing it.

OBJECTIVES

Students will:
● **think about how little they know about God;**
● **experience how communication is necessary for the development of a relationship;**
● **examine the importance Bible characters placed on developing their relationships with God;**
● **learn methods of personal Bible study they can use on their own; and**
● **commit themselves to study the Bible on a regular basis for a month.**

BIBLE BASIS

GENESIS 12:1-4
DANIEL 6:10-11
MATTHEW 14:13-14, 23

Look up the following scriptures. Then read the background paragraphs to see how the passages relate to your senior highers.

In **Genesis 12:1-4**, Abram leaves his home in obedience to God's command.

Here Abram demonstrates the strength of his relationship with God by setting out for an unknown land, simply at God's command. He listened to God's Word and obeyed it.

Junior highers need to see that reading God's Word isn't like a magical ritual that makes their days go better. It's part of growing a relationship with God that involves communication and obedience.

In **Daniel 6:10-11**, Daniel gets in trouble for his constant praying.

Daniel's dedication to his relationship with God was so strong that even his enemies knew about it. They knew he spent time with God in prayer three times daily. That's how they could catch him going against the king's order.

The dedication to God that Daniel showed in the face of death demonstrated the strength of his relationship with God. As kids study the Bible and grow closer to God, they too can develop relationships with God that'll support them in tough times.

In **Matthew 14:13-14, 23**, we see Jesus' example of spending time with God.

Even Jesus, the son of God, needed to spend time alone with God. Jesus' times in prayer gave him renewal, focus and challenge.

You and your kids each need time alone with God. And with the Bible, we have a tool to spark those quiet times: God has given us his message in written form.

THIS LESSON AT A GLANCE

Section	Minutes	What Students Will Do	Supplies
Opener (Option 1) (Option 2)	5 to 10	**The Voice of God**—Hold a God-sound-alike contest. **How Well Do You Know God?**—Take a quiz about God.	
Action and Reflection	10 to 15	**Incommunicado**—Try to get to know a partner without communicating.	
Bible Application	10 to 15	**Bible Discovery**—Practice using personal Bible-study methods.	Pencils, "Personal Bible Discovery" handouts (p. 42), Bibles
Commitment	5 to 10	**Commit to the Word**—Commit to explore the Bible regularly.	"Personal Bible Discovery" handouts (p. 42), pencils "Working on the Word" handouts (p. 43)
Closing (Option 1) (Option 2)	5 to 10	**Celebrate!**—Have a party celebrating God's gift of the Bible. **Quotable Quote**—Read quotes about understanding the Bible.	Party snacks, decorations

The Lesson

☐ OPTION 1: THE VOICE OF GOD

After everyone arrives, ask:

● **How do you think God sounds?**

Before kids respond, say: **We're going to hold a God-sound-alike contest.**

One by one, have kids come to the front of the room and say, "Let there be light!" in their best God-like voice. Don't give them any indication of what you expect God's voice to sound like.

When kids are finished, have them vote on whose God-voice sounded most like God.

Then ask:

● **How do we know what God sounds like?** (We imagine it from his power; we hear it in movies.)

● **Do you really think God speaks that way?** (Yes, he's big; no, he speaks softly.)

● **Most times God doesn't use an audible voice to get his message to us. How does God speak to us most often today?** (Through people; through the Bible.)

Say: **One of the most important ways God gets his message to us today is through the Bible. And to get those messages he wants us to have, we need to regularly read and study it. That's what our lesson is all about today.**

☐ OPTION 2: HOW WELL DO YOU KNOW GOD?

To begin your lesson, ask:

● **How well do you know God?**

Then say: **Let's take a quiz to measure how well we know God.**

Ask kids the following questions. The answers are in parentheses after the questions. Kids will probably have trouble answering all three questions.

Ask:

● **On which day of Creation did God create geese?** (Fifth; Genesis 1:20-23.)

● **How many names are used for God in the Old Testament?** (More than 15.)

● **When did Satan speak to God?** (When discussing Job; Job 1:6—2:6.)

When you've finished discussing the questions, say: **The answers to all those questions about God are in the Bible. And so are a lot of more important things we can learn about God. One very important reason we have for studying the Bible is to learn about God, which will help us grow in our relationship with him.**

INCOMMUNICADO

Have kids each pair up with the person in the room they know the least. Then say: **Sit down with your partner for two minutes to learn more about each other. There's only one catch: You can't talk to each other, write notes, touch each other or use any other communication. You must simply sit near each other.**

After two minutes of awkward silence and giggles, ask:

● **How much did you learn?** (Not much, since we couldn't talk; nothing, we needed to communicate.)

● **Is it possible to develop a relationship with someone without communication?** (No, you can't develop a relationship without learning about someone; no, you've got to be able to talk.)

● **Think about your relationship with the parent you're closest to. How would that relationship develop if you couldn't communicate in any way?** (It would be tough; we'd grow farther apart.)

● **How is trying to learn about each other without communicating like trying to develop a relationship with God without reading the Bible?** (You can't get to know God without taking in his Word; it's similar, but you can get to know God in other ways, too.)

● **To develop a close relationship with God, what do we need to do?** (Study the Bible; pray.)

Say: **God reveals himself to us through his Word. And to develop our relationship with God, we need to take in his Word by reading it. Let's look at how a few Bible characters worked on their relationships with God.**

BIBLE DISCOVERY

Give each person a pencil and a "Personal Bible Discovery" handout (p. 42). Form three groups. If you have more than 15 kids, form more groups so no group has more than five people. Assign one of these passages to each group:

● Abram (Genesis 12:1-4)
● Daniel (Daniel 6:10-11)
● Jesus (Matthew 14:13-14, 23)

Have groups each use the handout to work through their passage. When groups are finished, have them each report their findings.

Then ask:

● **What have we learned from this study?** (How Bible characters worked on their relationship with God; how important it is to spend time alone with God; how we can get more out of personal Bible study.)

Help direct kids to come up with all of the above answers. They may come up with lots more too.

Say: **If it was important even to Jesus to stay in contact with God the Father, then think how important it must be for us too. As we stay in touch with God through his Word, our relationship with him will grow.**

ACTION AND REFLECTION
(10 to 15 minutes)

BIBLE APPLICATION
(10 to 15 minutes)

COMMITMENT
(5 to 10 minutes)

COMMIT TO THE WORD
Give kids more "Personal Bible Discovery" handouts; at least three to each student. Say: **We've spent a month studying about the Bible. If you haven't done so yet, it's time now to really start studying the Bible on your own. You can use these handouts to help you get started.**

Give kids pencils and "Working on the Word" handouts (p. 43). As you're doing that, say: **If you're each willing to read at least three verses a day, and work through them using the "Personal Bible Discovery" handouts, I'd like you to sign the "Working on the Word" commitment and return it to me. You can choose how many days a week you commit to; any number from one to seven. But if you commit to it, remember: It involves your relationship with God; you need to take the commitment seriously.**

As kids are considering their commitments, say: **I encourage you to start with the Gospel of John, since it's a fairly simple book with a powerful message. And don't limit yourself to three verses. Read until you come to a logical break in the passage.**

After a minute or two, say: **Whether you've made a commitment or not, give your sheet to me. For those of you who made commitments, I'll make a photocopy for myself and return the original to you. That way I can encourage you along the way.**

Be sure to keep kids' commitment sheets handy in the coming weeks, so you can call and encourage kids in their commitment to read the Bible regularly.

Have kids return to the pairs they formed for the Incommunicado activity. Give pairs two minutes to get to know each other a bit better—using real communication. Have kids finish by each telling their partner how they've appreciated getting to know him or her during this class.

Before moving on to your closing, offer to give kids more "Personal Bible Discovery" sheets if and when they need them. Suggest that kids hole-punch their sheets and keep them in a three-ring binder.

CLOSING
(5 to 10 minutes)

☐ OPTION 1: CELEBRATE!
Say: **Isn't it exciting that God, the creator of the universe, wants to communicate with us? Let's celebrate that God gave us the Bible!**

Break out party snacks and party decorations. Let kids celebrate together. Sing songs of praise and thanks. Close your time together by singing a familiar, favorite scripture song.

☐ OPTION 2: QUOTABLE QUOTE
Read aloud this quote from Mark Twain: **"Most people are bothered by those passages in scripture which they can-**

not understand; but as for me, I always noticed that the passages in scripture which trouble me most are those which I do understand."

You may want to read the quote again for understanding and emphasis, or copy it onto newsprint for all to see.

Ask:

● **What is Mark Twain saying in this quote?** (When we understand scripture, sometimes we're troubled because we aren't obeying it.)

● **What's one thing you've understood in this course that challenges you?**

● **What will you do in response to that challenge?**

Close with prayer, asking God to help kids apply to their lives what they learn in the Bible.

If You Still Have Time . . .

Show and Tell—Before your class, use the "Personal Bible Discovery" handout once in your own personal Bible study. Then in class, walk through it with kids, showing them what you discovered and how you'll apply it to your life.

Course Reflection—Form a circle. Ask students to reflect on the past four lessons. Have them take turns completing the following sentences:

● Something I learned in this course was . . .

● If I could tell my friends about this course, I'd say . . .

● Something I'll do differently because of this course is . . .

Personal Bible Discovery

Use the four questions on this sheet to help you study your assigned passage. Then keep the questions to help you in your own personal Bible study.

Passage _____

What's it say?

(In a nutshell, what's the message of this passage?)

What's it mean?

(What does this passage suggest people should do to respond?)

What's it mean to me?

(How does this passage apply to me?)

What am I going to do about it?

(What will I do in response to the message of this passage?)

WORKING ON THE

To develop my relationship with God, I commit to read and carefully study a scripture passage of at least three verses each day, _____ day(s) of the week. I promise to follow through on this commitment the best I can for the next four weeks.

Signed _____

BONUS IDEAS

Biblical Literature 101—Study the way God uses various types of literature in the Bible to speak to his people. Look at sections of the Bible that contain history (Genesis), poetry (Psalms), wisdom literature (Proverbs), epistles (Romans) and prophecy (Isaiah).

Translation Clarification—Have your pastor or a Bible scholar come to your class to discuss various Bible translations available today. Be sure your guest explains the difference between a translation and a paraphrase, and discusses the value of different types of translations for different purposes.

Jesus and the Old Testament—Help kids take a look at how Jesus used the scriptures available to him in his ministry. Study the gospels, and evaluate Jesus' opinion of the Old Testament.

Bible Baseball—Play Bible Baseball with your kids. Form two teams, and quiz kids on Bible content using questions of four difficulty levels. Question cards from Bible-trivia games work well. Kids each get to choose what level question they want to try for. A correct answer to the easiest level means a one-base hit; a correct answer to the hardest level means a home run. A wrong answer receives an out. Play as many innings as you have time for.

You may also want to create variations for basketball, football or any other sport.

Evidence That Demands Belief—Lead your kids in a study of the reliability of the Bible. Help them see how archaeology and historical writings support what the Bible says. Good sources to build this study on are *Evidence That Demands a Verdict* by Josh McDowell (Here's Life), *Who Moved the Stone?* by Frank Morison (Zondervan), and the magazine Biblical Archaeology Review. Check your local public library.

Into the Word—After completing this course on the Bible, your kids might be ready to launch into a Bible study just for them. Consider setting up an hour sometime during the week when you or another youth leader or teacher can get together with the junior highers to lead them in a Bible study. Let kids help choose the topic or book to study, and consider letting kids lead the study once in a while.

MEETINGS AND MORE

Table Talk—Use the "Table Talk" handout (p. 19) as the basis for a meeting for your junior highers and their parents. You might want to meet following the last lesson of this course. Provide activities that promote interaction between parents and kids. For ideas, check *Quick Crowdbreakers and Games for Youth Groups* (Group). Sometime during the meeting, have kids and parents work through the "Table Talk" handout together. At the end, have people tell what they discovered through their discussions.

Giving It Away—Once your kids have seen the importance of the Bible, they'll be more interested in getting it into the hands of people who don't have it. Suggest that kids give Bibles or money to an agency that delivers Bibles to other parts of the world. You could even do a fund-raiser with that goal in mind. Contact agencies such as the American Bible Society, 1865 Broadway, New York, NY 10023, or Wycliffe Bible Translators, Box 2727, Huntington Beach, CA 92647.

Giving It Away, Version 2—If your kids grasp the significance of having God's Word in their hands and his Holy Spirit living within them, they may get excited about telling their friends about their faith. Talking about their faith will still be scary for kids, but you can help them do it. Use the "Putting It All Together" handout (p. 48), to help kids plan how to tell friends the message of eternal life in Jesus Christ. Then encourage them to take advantage of opportunities that come along. And don't forget to pray for them and their efforts.

PARTY PLEASERS

Real Characters—Have a costume party where kids come dressed as Bible characters. Give prizes for the most authentic-looking costume, the character the most kids guess correctly, the most obscure Bible character, the craziest Bible character, and any other fun winners you come up with. Serve foods similar to those in Bible times: dried fruits and meats, biscuits and honey, and grape juice.

Bible Game Night—Plan a party around Bible games. You could use Bible Baseball or other games. Or use any of the Bible-trivia games available. But be warned: Most of the trivia games are extremely tough.

For another option, create your own Bible games, basing them on game shows like *Jeopardy* or *Hollywood Squares*.

Bible Body-Building—Use a retreat to help your kids begin to do their own personal Bible study. Do retreat meetings that help kids get into the Word on their own. Get them started using the "Personal Bible Discovery" handouts (p. 42) or any other method you've found to be effective.

Be sure to have lots of fun on the retreat, too. Plan an activity around finding humor in the Bible, and give kids a chance to play Bible games. Make the retreat a time kids can enjoy while still learning to exercise their Bible-study "muscles."

RETREAT IDEA

PUTTING IT ALL TOGETHER

Complete this handout to help you plan what to say to someone who's interested in your faith.

1. What role does Jesus play in your life on a day-to-day basis?

2. When did your relationship with Jesus begin?

3. How has your relationship with Jesus grown?

4. How does the Bible help you?

5. How does your faith help you face the future?

6. Key verses you can use in presenting God's message of eternal life in Christ are John 3:16, Romans 3:23; and Romans 6:23. Read each verse and work with your leader to write how you might explain God's message to a friend.

...cal church use. Copyright © Group Publishing, Inc., Box 481, Loveland, CO 80539.